SUPPLIES

If you're just starting your coloring adventure, get ready for a whole new world of discovery! From markers and colored pencils to gel pens and pastels, today's coloring supplies offer colorists plenty of opportunities to play, experiment, and create stunning works of art. You can find basic coloring supplies at almost any store, which makes it convenient to get started.

Coloring supplies can range in price from economical to artist-quality expensive. While a higher price point often yields higher quality, if you're just getting started and you're on a budget, don't get too hung up on brands. Instead, experiment with whatever supplies you can afford as you practice coloring the designs in this book. When you use the right techniques, even the cheapest coloring supplies can yield dazzling works of art! Then, when you're ready, you can add more expensive brands to your cache of supplies.

Colored Pencils

Colored pencils are an attractive choice for coloring because they can be used to achieve vibrant blends, subtle shading, and beautiful details, and they also tend to be more forgiving than markers and other media. While it typically takes longer to color with colored pencils than it does with markers, the luminous results can make the effort totally worth it! There are plenty of colored pencil options on the market, and it all comes down to what feels right for you. Here are some things to think about when you set out to purchase colored pencils.

Many colored pencil brands offer two different types of pencils: inexpensive student-quality pencils and artist-quality (also called professional-quality) pencils that cost more but contain higher pigment content, resulting in richer, more vivid colors. If you decide to purchase artist-quality colored pencils, your next consideration will be whether to get oil-based pencils or wax-based pencils. Student-quality pencils are typically only wax-based. Before you purchase your colored pencils, be sure to check the label to see whether they are student-grade or artist-grade, because there can be a noticeable difference in quality and user experience.

When you use colored pencils, you can easily achieve vibrant results that seamlessly blend together.

> ### Tip
>
> A kneaded eraser is a good choice when trying to erase colored pencil.

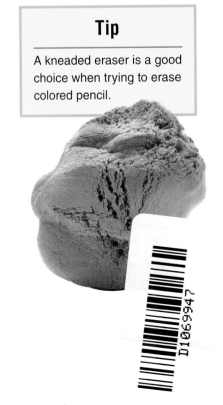

D1069947

Markers

The markers most commonly used for coloring are either alcohol-based or water-based. (Oil-based markers are geared toward surfaces other than paper.) Water-based marker colors can be diluted with water, while alcohol-based markers can be blended by layering colors or using rubbing alcohol. (A colorless blender marker will help you achieve results with both types of marker.) One advantage to using alcohol-based markers is that they will not warp or buckle thinner paper the way water-based markers do.

Dual-tip markers, like these water-based brush markers from Tombow, give you a lot of flexibility and control in a single marker.

Tip

Markers sometimes bleed through your coloring pages. One trick to help with this is to put a scrap page underneath your design, which will catch any bleed-through and prevent it from getting onto other coloring pages or your table. Another trick is to spray hairspray or another fixative onto your blank page before you color it with markers. This will minimize marker bleed-through . . . but test it on a sample page first!

When outlining, color slightly inside the line to allow for ink bleed. In the image above, the center petal was colored not quite up to the black line, and bled up to it nicely. The petal to the right was colored right up to the black line, and bled over it.

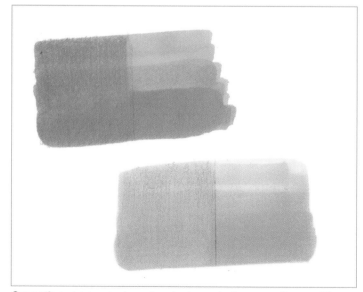

Smooth out any marker streaks by coloring over them with a matching colored pencil. The left sides were colored over with colored pencil.

Gel Pens

Gel pens are perfect for enhancing and embellishing colored pieces. Because they are pens with fine-tip points, coloring an entire page with them would be very time consuming; however, gel pens can be used to accentuate smaller areas in many unique and fun ways. Because of their unique ink, gel pens produce colors with a different tone and quality than markers and colored pencils. Try using them to add little pops of neon or other vibrant colors to a piece you've completed with markers or colored pencils.

Blue metallic on a blue base—not so great.

Gold glitter on a lilac base—it works!

Yellow glaze pen on an orange base—doesn't work.

Use slow, steady strokes to avoid line skipping.

Tip

Gel pens are awesome detailers because they are opaque in nature, but they do require a little bit of experimentation; some tones will not show up well when layered on top of dark base shades.

Allow time for the ink to dry to avoid smears—try working in the direction of your dominant hand (if you're right-handed, from left to right).

Crayons

Pretty much everyone can remember coloring when they were younger with a good old box of crayons. After all, they are the quintessential children's coloring tool. Unfortunately, they're not generally suited for creating polished, professional-looking pieces.

The good thing about crayons is that they are incredibly affordable and they come in a massive range of colors for very little investment. You can also get crayons that come in pencil form now, such as Crayola Twistables®. Some adults find coloring with traditional crayons either childish or difficult (due to the short length of the crayons), so these pencil-like crayons can help with that.

Overall, for a beginning colorist or someone who just likes the nostalgia of coloring with crayons, they can be a good investment. Just don't expect polished results without quite a bit of effort.

Crayons have their own unique textured effect.

Watercolors

There are many different techniques for using watercolors. You can use a lot of water and a little bit of color to make a pretty, ethereal wash of color on an entire page or a large section of a design, and then color or create a pattern on top of that. You can also use very little water for a drybrush effect, which can create interesting textures and a more vivid color payoff. You can put water on the paper first and then bleed color into it, and you can also do it the other way around, laying down a somewhat dry swath of color and then adding more water to it to blend it out. You can blend your watercolors together to make new colors either directly on the paper or separately on a palette. The possibilities are endless!

Watercolor in Coloring Books

Because coloring book pages tend to be on the thin side, most won't hold up to more than a little water. To eliminate this problem, copy the coloring page design onto heavier watercolor paper. If you want to use the paper that came in your coloring book, it is best to tear it out of the book to prevent ruining any pages underneath it. Paint a few test swatches on an inconspicuous corner of the paper to see how the paper reacts.

COLOR THEORY

Let's start with the color wheel. This simple tool is the basis for everything you need to know to get started exploring color. I'll use this familiar tool to explain different color categories, relationships, and combinations to help you learn your way around color and color schemes. It's easy for beginners to feel overwhelmed by the sheer volume of colors that their colored pencil or marker sets offer, but a basic understanding of the color wheel and color terminology will help you make use of the thousands of different colors out there.

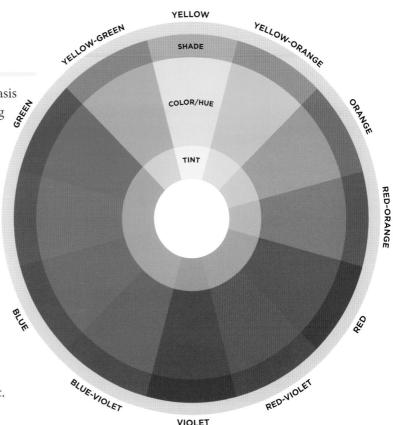

Basic Color Categories

The color wheel can be divided up into many different, helpful "sets" of colors. First, let's explore the most basic.

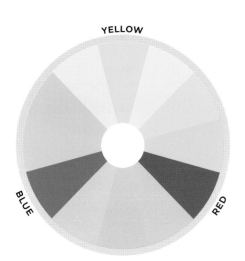

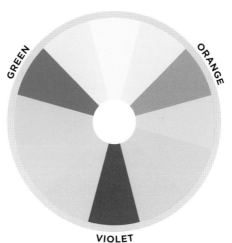

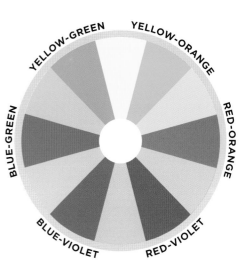

Primary Colors

The three primary colors—red, yellow, and blue—can't be created by mixing any other colors together and are the basis for creating the rest of the colors on the color wheel.

Secondary Colors

The secondary colors are orange, green, and violet (often called purple). They are created by mixing two primary colors together. Mixing the primary colors red and blue creates violet; mixing red and yellow creates orange; mixing blue and yellow creates green.

Tertiary Colors

Tertiary colors are created by mixing a primary (p) color with one of its adjacent secondary (s) colors. For example. mixing red (p) and violet (s) creates the tertiary color red-violet (magenta).

Color Schemes

Now that we've covered the basics of the color wheel, let's talk about color schemes. Color schemes are what we call the combinations of various colors from the color wheel in a piece of artwork. Picking a color scheme from these options is a great way to get started with a piece of art and know that your colors will work well together, but don't be afraid to break away from these models, either. Many great works of art combine all sorts of colors, including all the colors of the rainbow!

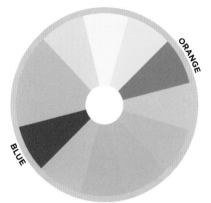

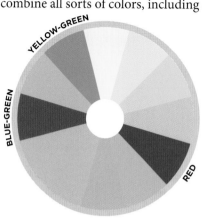

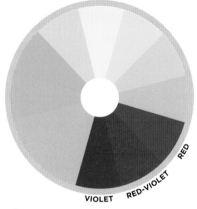

Complementary Colors

Complementary colors are directly opposite each other on the color wheel, such as blue and orange.

Split Complementary Colors

A split complementary color scheme is made up of a color plus the two colors adjacent to its complement. For example, a split complementary scheme might include red, teal (blue-green), and chartreuse (yellow-green).

Analogous Colors

Analogous color schemes use colors that are right next to each other on the color wheel, often in sets of three, and have a very harmonious effect. For instance, violet, magenta (red-violet), and red are analogous.

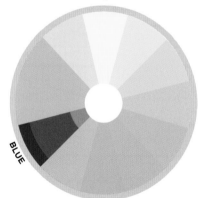

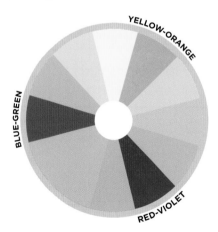

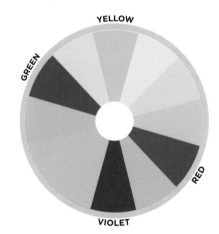

Monochromatic Colors

If you don't want to think too hard or want to go really simple with your color scheme, try a monochromatic look. Pick a single color, such as blue, and then pull out every blue coloring utensil you have and color with it.

Triadic Colors

If you can imagine an equilateral triangle superimposed on top of the color wheel, the three colors it touches form a triadic color scheme. For example, amber (yellow-orange), magenta (red-violet), and teal (blue-green) are a triad.

Tetradic Colors

Tetradic color schemes are made up of two pairs of complementary colors; imagine a skinny rectangle superimposed on the color wheel. A tetradic color scheme might consist of yellow, violet, red, and green.

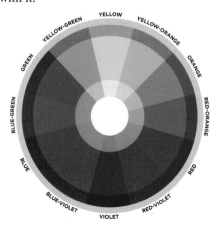

Warm and Cool Colors

Warm colors include most red- and yellow-based colors and tend to convey feelings of warmth, energy, and brightness. Cool colors include most blue- and green-based colors and tend to convey feelings of calm, coolness, and depth.

TECHNIQUES

Shading

When shading, you need to decide what tools and methods you want to use. There are four general methods. The first method—the single-color, two-tool method—creates the most realistic effect.

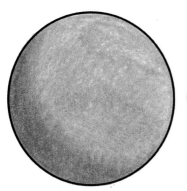  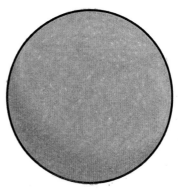 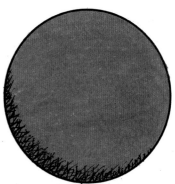

Method 1: Pick two similar shades from the same color family and use them together: a base color (lighter color) and a shade color (darker color).

Method 2: Use varying degrees of pressure with a single coloring tool to make the shaded part darker than the rest.

Method 3: Add black or gray where you want shading, or use a totally different color than the one you're using as a base.

Method 4: Use line techniques like stippling or crosshatching.

Highlighting

A simple way to add highlights to your coloring is to use a white gel pen (for severe highlights) or white colored pencil (for subtle highlights). You could also use a kneaded eraser to pick up some of the base color where you would like to place a highlight; this works best with colored pencils. With a little planning, you can simply leave an area uncolored from the beginning to create a highlight.

 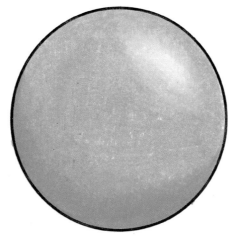 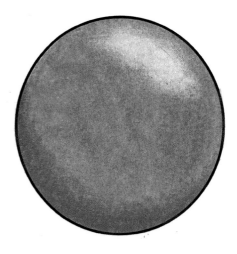

Gel pen highlight

Colored pencil highlight

Highlight created by erasing

Blending

Blending allows you to seamlessly combine colors together to create visually stunning art. When blending, you can use any colors or media you want. We recommend starting with a monochromatic color scheme in one specific medium until you get comfortable with the process. Colored pencils are good tools for beginners to learn blending.

Tip

With dry tools, like crayons and colored pencils, tool sharpness and hand pressure make all the difference. With wet tools, these two things are not a factor. Simply layer colors one over another, back and forth.

1. Base

2. Add

3. Blend

Start by laying down the light base color over the entire area you want to blend.

Use the dark shade to color lightly from the middle of the base color toward one edge of the shape. As you move farther away from the area of your base shade, begin adding more pressure to your pencil, coloring the area more heavily.

Go back with the light base color and color over the base and dark shade areas. Repeat until you've created a nice, even coat of color.

Blending with Wet Tools

Wet tools, like markers and watercolors, will simply need to be layered over one another, back and forth, to achieve blended colors.

Colored pencils. Color by Jill Rogers. Design on page 19.

Markers. Color by Malia Skidmore. Design on page 33.

Markers. Color by Malia Skidmore. Design on page 35.

Colored pencils. Color by Jill Rogers. Design on page 65.

Colored pencils. Color by Jill Rogers. Design on page 39.

Markers. Color by Malia Skidmore. Design on page 79.

Colored pencils. Color by Jill Rogers. Design on page 73.

Markers. Color by Malia Skidmore. Design on page 63.

© Design Originals. www.D-Originals.com

I don't ask for the meaning of the
song of a bird or the rising of the sun
on a misty morning. There they are,
and they are beautiful.

—Pete Hamill

A quiet secluded life in the country,
with the possibility of being useful to
people to whom it is easy to do good
… such is my idea of happiness.

—Leo Tolstoy

© Design Originals. www.D-Originals.com

How lucky country children are in these natural delights that lie ready to their hand! Every season and every plant offers changing joys.

—Miss Read

© Design Originals, www.D-Originals.com

Some old-fashioned things like fresh
air and sunshine are hard to beat.

—Laura Ingalls Wilder

© Design Originals, www.D-Originals.com

I like old bookstores, the smell of coffee brewing, rainy day naps, farmhouse porches, and sunsets. I like the sweet, simple things that remind me that life doesn't have to be complicated to be beautiful.

—Brooke Hampton

© Design Originals, www.D-Originals.com

To me, flowers are happiness.

—Stefano Gabbana

Home is the nicest word there is.

—Laura Ingalls Wilder

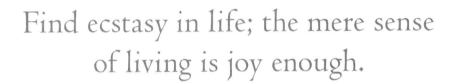

Find ecstasy in life; the mere sense
of living is joy enough.

—Emily Dickinson

If I hadn't started painting, I would
have raised chickens.

—Grandma Moses

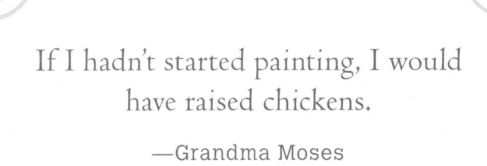

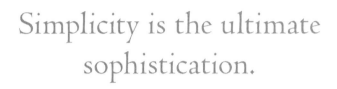

Simplicity is the ultimate
sophistication.

—Leonardo da Vinci

© Design Originals, www.d-originals.com

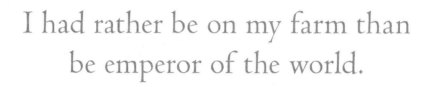

I had rather be on my farm than
be emperor of the world.

—George Washington

© Design Originals. www.D-Originals.com

Flowers always make people
better, happier, and more hopeful;
they are sunshine, food, and
medicine for the soul.

—Luther Burbank

Snowflakes swirl down gently in the deep blue haze beyond the window. The outside world is a dream. Inside, the fireplace is brightly lit, and the Yule log crackles with orange and crimson sparks.

—Vera Nazarian

© Design Originals. www.D-Originals.com

To lie sometimes on the grass under trees on a summer's day, listening to the murmur of the water, or watching the clouds float across the sky, is by no means a waste of time.

—John Lubbock

A happy life must be to a great extent a quiet life, for it is only in an atmosphere of quiet that true joy dare live.

—Bertrand Russell

A sunflower field is like a sky
with a thousand suns.

—Corina Abdulahm-Negura

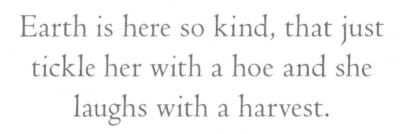

Earth is here so kind, that just tickle her with a hoe and she laughs with a harvest.

—Douglas Jerrold

If you look the right way, you can see
that the whole world is a garden.

—Frances Hodgson Burnett

© Design Originals. www.D-Originals.com

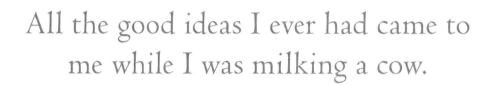

All the good ideas I ever had came to me while I was milking a cow.

—Grant Wood

True friends are like bright sunflowers
that never fade away, even over
distance and time.

—Marie Williams Johnstone

© Design Originals. www.D-Originals.com

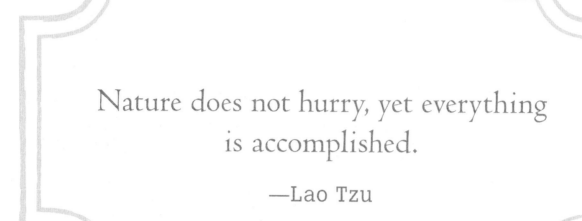

Nature does not hurry, yet everything is accomplished.

—Lao Tzu

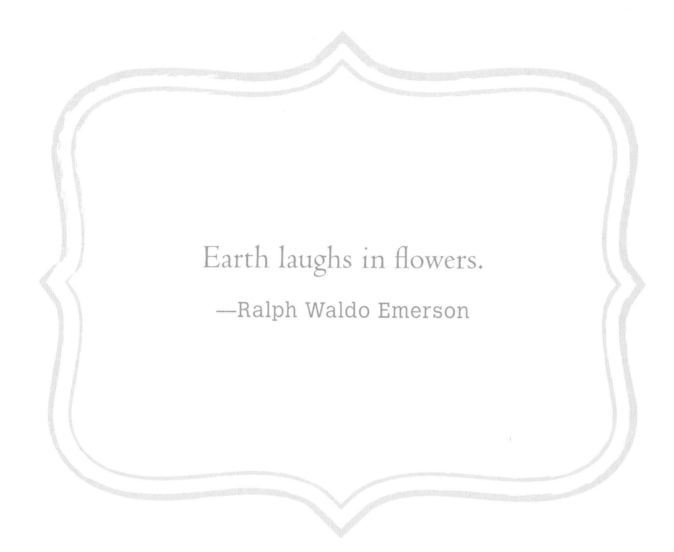

Earth laughs in flowers.

—Ralph Waldo Emerson

Rest and be thankful.

—William Wordsworth

Of all the paths you take in life, make
sure a few of them are dirt.

—John Muir

© Design Originals. www.d-originals.com

I am fond of pigs. Dogs look up
to us. Cats look down on us.
Pigs treat us as equals.

—Winston S. Churchill

© Design Originals. www.D-Originals.com

Winter is the time for comfort, for good food and warmth, for the touch of a friendly hand and for a talk beside the fire: it is the time for home.

—Edith Sitwell

© Design Originals. www.D-Originals.com

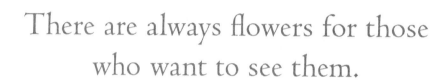

There are always flowers for those
who want to see them.

—Henri Matisse

© Design Originals. www.D-Originals.com

If a year was tucked inside of a
clock, then autumn would be
the magic hour.

—Victoria Erickson

© Design Originals. www.D-Originals.com

Peace is always beautiful.

—Walt Whitman

© Design Originals. www.D-Originals.com

Summer afternoon—summer afternoon; to me those have always been the two most beautiful words in the English language.

—Henry James

© Design Originals, www.D-Originals.com

Autumn carries more gold in its pocket than all the other seasons.

—Jim Bishop

To plant a garden is to
believe in tomorrow.

—Audrey Hepburn